YOUR ASSERTIVE LIFE SERIES

HAPPINESS
UPGRADE

6 Steps to Finding Greater Joy, Success, and
Advantage on Your Way to Living A More Fulfilling Life

YOUR ASSERTIVE LIFE SERIES

HAPPINESS
UPGRADE

6 Steps to Finding Greater Joy, Success, and Advantage on Your Way to Living A More Fulfilling Life

Written By:
Andy Raingold

Graphic Design By: Stephen Hawkins.
Special Thanks to Nathanial Dasco & Ikhide Oshoma - Natalie and Joeel Rivera (Transformational Academy)

ThinkeLife Publications

Andy Raingold - www.andyraingold.com
Visit my website at www.upgradeyourhappiness.com

First printing: August 2020.

ISBN: 978 1 913929 73 2

Table of Contents

Introduction

Do you find it difficult to be happy because of your stature or the general conditions in your life, or because of problems plaguing you?

Have you attained all the luxuries or achievements in the world, but still feel unhappy?

Do you feel that something is missing, that you're incomplete, that there's a big empty space waiting to be filled in your life?

Have you tried everything you can to find a sense of joy and purpose in your life, but failed every single time?

If so, then this book holds the key that could actually cure all your problems and heartaches! Or ease them at the very least.

Some people work all their lives to reach their heart's desires yet you may be shocked to know that even though they have reached the highest peaks of accomplishment, they are still unhappy. Why is this so?

Happiness is abstract. It cannot be seen nor touched. It can only be felt and experienced. Happiness encompasses the feeling of completion, contentment, and inner peace. And in the end, this is everyone's real goal whether they acknowledge or are even aware of it or not.

"If you are armed with the proper knowledge, you can achieve happiness with what you have and with what you currently are."

As a person who is focused on living your life fully, you still might wonder why happiness seems to be so elusive. You always do what you have to do, and you do it the right way to reach your goals. You might have even achieved countless qualifications, certificates, medals, recognition, and wealth. But why can't any of these give you the happiness you may be seeking?

Well, we have the answers for you within this little book!

What you are about to learn will change your life forever if, you come to fully understand the foundation of all success and true happiness as discussed in part two, and then follow the practical steps given in part three of this book.

You are not simply going to be happy for a limited period. You are going to stay extremely happy for the rest of your life! In fact, as long as you follow this process you will continue to build greater happiness over time!

It is everyone's dream to be content and happy with life which is usually the main reason why most of us do the things that we do. You want to be able to sleep well at night feeling satisfied as you reflect on how you are moving forward, making progress, and eventually accomplishing your goals. And who wouldn't want to wake up every morning with a light, sunny, and energized feeling of contentment and self-satisfaction knowing you are progressing towards your dreams in a state of growing joy?

You most likely think of things and do almost everything it takes to be happier and so you expect happiness to follow as an effect of every successful venture.

And it often does! But most of the time, happiness always seems to be short-lived. Happiness seems to come and go all too easily. It never really stays for good. And as the happy feelings fade, you are left with nothing but a vacuum of unfulfilled and unrealized feelings.

At times, it really doesn't matter who you are and what you have. Happiness can be as evasive both to the wealthy and the average

Person and so being sad is an all too common reality. And it can strike anybody and everybody at any time.

But the good news is...

"You can achieve happiness now. Happiness is within you. All you have to do is harness that inner joy and happiness present in all of us. And you can do it in so many simple yet overlooked ways."

Did you know that you can still be happy despite encountering the seemingly unlimited number of challenges or hardships in life?

You can use your body and your mind to become happy at any moment. And although there are people who can lead you towards greater happiness in life, mainly through experiences and external stimuli. You can be much happier on your own and through your own efforts!

Genuinely happy people have problems like everyone else on earth. They experience difficulties just like everybody else, maybe even more so? But they are able to overcome them. They are equipped with the knowledge and outlook in life that get them through obstacles and challenges and you can have that too!

This book will lead you through a six-step process to increase your happiness every day. It will help you discover the unique secrets of a truly happy person. And you can conveniently apply these concepts to your everyday life!

The Happiness Upgrade will show you how you can be happy every single day of your life no matter what comes your way.

Inside this book you will discover:

- **The Three Steps to Succeed at Anything:** That allows you to get more of what you want from life and helps you to build your perfect life with greater confidence in the outcomes you'll experience over time.

- **Your Three Life's:** That is the foundation of yourself, your life, and all things in existence, and that allows you to completely understand where you are and where you've been. When you begin to look at life through this secret you will begin to succeed at everything that you do. You cannot fail when you take this kind of control of your life, except by your own choice?

- **The Six Layers That Block Your Happiness:** That helps you to become more aware of the things you do that block your joy, then shows you how you can cultivate progressively more happiness in an enjoyable, fun way.

- **How to Upgrade Your Happiness:** Through simple steps that help you to experience much greater happiness and elevate yourself from where you are right now to a place of true lasting happiness that grows without end.

- **The Physiology of Happiness:** That gives you a complete understanding of how happiness works and enables you to breed happiness into your very being exponentially as you systematically remove each happiness block.

And a whole lot of other enriching and enlightening points to help you live life in the happiest state possible.

Happiness doesn't simply happen. It can be made to happen. You just need to understand part two and practice part three of this book to take your first steps to greater joy in life.

Andy Raingold

PART 1:

Happiness 101: Overview

Is Happiness Even Possible?

Though the question above is inherently ominous, it is still one that every person on the planet should ask themselves at one point in their lives, or ultimately face the resulting consequences. The unfortunate reality is that happiness eludes most people on the planet, though you would be hard-pressed to find someone who is not seeking it. But the pursuit of happiness must begin with the first step: believing that it is possible.

The trap that too many fall into is that this life is not designed for people to achieve happiness. One only needs to turn on the news to be overwhelmed with the tragedies that are occurring almost every minute of every day. However, what the news fails to report on are the millions of people that are living a happy and fulfilled life. So, what is the difference between so many who are living happily and the masses of people who are not? Well, there are quite a few, many of which we will discuss here, but the primary starting point is that those who live happily, believe that they can do so.

"Indeed, man wishes to be happy even when he lives as to make happiness impossible" – St. Augustine

Once you realize that the way in which you are living is the problem, you will be able to realize that happiness is possible. However, it is not a gift that is just given from above for the vast majority of people. In order to be truly happy most of the time, it is your lifestyle and your thoughts that need changing. Once they are changed, happiness can begin to flourish in all areas of your life. So, are you ready to believe?

Happiness and The Purpose of Life

We mentioned before that people fall into traps when it comes to happiness, and there is likely no bigger mistake that mankind makes than to believe happiness is the purpose of life. Because so many people seek it, yet do not have it, it makes logical sense that they would pursue happiness in and of itself as a goal or a destination. This leads many people to fall into destructive behavior such as excessive gambling, alcohol, drug addiction, sex addictions, or getting into unhealthy relationships. The reason people often do this is that the associated pleasure that many of these stimulants provide can be mistaken for true happiness and so people make them their lives pursuit.

Attempting to obtain happiness in this way is a disaster waiting to happen. Happiness, rather than an experience of pleasure, is better seen as a by-product of a successful life and we will dig into how to do that in part three of this book. For now, the two, a great life and happiness, are inherently intertwined and cannot be truly separated. Happiness can act as a platform by which you are able to gain success in life, however more on that specific topic later. For now, it is important to realize that along the journey is where happiness is found, not necessarily in specific destinations.

So, in order to be happy, it is important for you to find a purpose in life that is not directly the pursuit of happiness. If you find yourself excessively using external sources of stimulation, for example, pornography or drugs, it may be that you are not working towards a purpose in life which is in turn hindering your ability to be naturally happy. There is no easy way to discover your purpose in life, and for that reason, I created The Better Life Experience Program available through the firstlevel.vip website and mentioned at the back of this book. However, all humans have intrinsic desires, abilities, and passions.

Through inner searching, it is possible to find the common ground between these three building blocks and find a purpose for yourself. Perhaps you could use your love for fishing and your skill as a teacher to create the world's largest angling academy? Or maybe you can take your passion for F1 and your skills in a caring environment to create a charity that gives disabled children race car experiences? The possibilities are endless when it comes to purpose, as long as there is a passion and/or a need. However, once you have that purpose and are actively pursuing it, it is likely that happiness will not be far away.

Self-Sacrifice and Happiness

The idea of self-sacrifice has unfortunately become overly romanticized and distorted through stories and other mediums. In our current era, there is an epidemic of problematic self-sacrifice that actually leads to far more harm than it does good, especially in the arena of happiness. But how can all of this be true if self-sacrifice is usually seen as a noble thing? The problem arises when the sacrifice comes at the cost of your happiness and is systemic rather than the occasional choice. Allow me to explain.

Imagine two different people Amy and Steve. Both of these people are part of the same ultimate Frisbee club. As part of their training a lot of equipment, such as hoops and hurdles are brought to every practice but the equipment is not small and needs to be delivered by vehicle. The club decides to hold a vote on how best to deal with this issue. Amy, who believes that self-sacrifice is the best way to happiness decides to volunteer to be the one to bring the equipment to practice every week. Steve on the other hand thinks that members should take turns in keeping and transporting the equipment. However, because the members think it would be easier to just let Amy handle the task, the vote goes in her favor.

After a few months of being in charge of keeping and transporting the equipment, Amy is starting to find that she dreads going to practice. Every time she goes to get ready, she has to go to her garage, drag out the heavy and sizeable equipment, and attempt to store it in her car. She also has to turn up earlier than everyone else because the equipment needs to be set up and laid out ahead of time. To add to her misery, she is also the last to leave as she has to collect the equipment, bring it to her car and then store it before she gets home. Amy has begun to realize that she is no longer enjoying ultimate Frisbee and begins to consider giving up the sport she loved because she did not realize her unhappiness is coming from systemic self-sacrifice.

If the club had decided to go with Steve's suggestion then Amy would still have had the chance to occasionally volunteer to take the equipment without making it solely her responsibility. In this way, she would have still been able to sacrifice, whenever she would volunteer, but it would have been on her terms and would therefore not have been so detrimental to her own happiness. Dr. Pikiewicz (2015) writes in Psychology Today that trying to make everyone happy is bound to make yourself miserable. Therefore, if you are constantly trying to self-sacrifice to become happy, it may be time for a new approach.

There is also another way in which happiness and self-sacrifice have a difficult relationship, and that comes in the form of sacrificing ourselves to obtain happiness. This point links back to the earlier concept of people making the feeling of pleasure their primary pursuit of happiness and therefore experience a host of negative consequences. Sacrificing yourself for the pursuit of happiness is the logical expansion of that point.

Many people are desperate for happiness, especially in the western world. According to the World Health Organization around 264 million people suffer from depression worldwide and the disorder is common in all ages and genders. And because depression and a lack of happiness are so detrimental to our human experience people are willing to give up a lot in its pursuit.

Take for example the depressed factory worker who takes his weekly wages down to the local betting shop in order to make a quick profit but finds himself losing far more than he ever wins.

This person is sacrificing his financial stability in order to obtain happiness. Yet each loss piles a small piece of negative energy in his mind which grows to massive proportions over time.

Another example could be the girl that continuously goes back to her bad abusive boyfriend. Even though she knows that their relationship is toxic, it has given her a false sense of intimacy which, because of childhood traumas, makes her feel temporarily happy whenever she is with him. In this case, the girl is sacrificing her mental and possibly physical safety by trying to obtain her happiness from such negative external sources.

The moral of the story is that the pursuit of happiness should not come at the expense of sacrificing other extremely important areas in your life. There are ways and methods to become happy where you will not have to engage in behavior that is self-destructive and can actually enhance the lives of you and those around you.

Success and Happiness

What Is the Exact Meaning of Success and Happiness?

While it may be difficult to define success and happiness, it is not impossible. However, it has to be kept in mind that these terms can be slightly relative depending on who you ask. People often measure success in a million different ways but studies have shown us that there are a few indicators that people link towards success more than anything else.

One of these ways is financial freedom. While an obsession with money can certainly have detrimental effects on your happiness it is true that many people worry about money, according to YourMoney, the figure reaches 9.5 million in the UK alone (2019).

This is a shocking amount of people that have a difficult time being happy because of a lack of finances. However, is the key to being happy in regards to financial success simply about having a lot of money? It does not quite seem to be so. Research has found that there is a cut-off point after which gaining more resources does not equate to being happier. This means that financial success only has the ability to affect our happiness to a certain degree.

The way money makes you happy can be two-fold. Firstly, when you receive a paycheck or financial reward of any kind your brain releases dopamine. This is part of its reward system made up of neurotransmitter molecules in your brain as well as receptor sites to which these molecules bind. When dopamine is released and binds to its receptor it makes you feel good (this is the reason things like cocaine and gambling are often viewed as pleasurable experiences).

The second way money can make you happy is because it opens up more freedom of choice. Someone who has a large number of resources has the ability to make more spur of the moment decisions, like going on holidays, eating out at restaurants, or visiting establishments for entertainment such as theatres or go-kart tracks. Because of this increased level of freedom people with more money tend to be happier than the average person on a working-class salary. This means that financial success, at least to a certain degree, is inexplicably linked to an increase in happiness despite the contrary being used as a common phrase or words of wisdom.

Another measure of success is social status. While it may seem counterintuitive for many people to see their social lives as being something that can be successful and unsuccessful, it is still very common for people to measure their success in the amount, and type, of people they are surrounded with. Again, nuance is the key element of a successful social status as many go for a quantitative approach, i.e. the more friends and acquaintances they have the more successful they see themselves. While others prefer to measure their social success in the net-worth of the people they surround themselves with instead.

In 2012 the Huffington Post reported that new research by the British National Child Development Study or NCDS concluded that having a large friendship circle is directly correlated to a better sense of wellbeing, or happiness, in middle-aged people. This research indicates that the quantitative approach mentioned earlier may be more beneficial when looking at the link between social success and happiness. It is also interesting to note that in the study it was found that people usually had larger friendship circles if they did not enter higher or advanced forms of education. However, this is not a suggestion to stop learning.

In the end, it is undeniable that success and happiness are linked. Their definitions, however, seem to be more fluid than one would expect, and certain measures used to define them can often change depending on the circumstance and type of success one is measuring. In light of this, it is possibly best to simply ask yourself of your personal definition of success and happiness rather than looking for an objective one.

Being Honest About Your Level of Happiness

This last point leads us to something that maybe even more important than knowing the definition of happiness, and that is, to be honest with yourself about just how happy you really are. Though you may think this to be a redundant point, it is far more important than you may first realize.

Take for example the continuing rise of social media. Just a decade ago the figures for social media users were drastically smaller than it is today. And because of the increasing use of social media, there is an added pressure for people to present their lives in a certain way. According to Science Daily (2014), people fake many things they post on social media to create a certain type of image. And more often than not what is being faked, is a general level of happiness.

Because self-deception is climbing rapidly it is important to be vigilant in your measures when it comes to this subject. While it may be uncomfortable to admit you should know whether or not you are faking your level of happiness to someone else, such as a spouse or the people who follow you on social media, or if you are lying to yourself. Here are a few simple questions you can ask yourself that may make this process easier for you:

1. Do you often feel negative emotions when posting on social media?
2. Do you ever feel like you smile when you do not feel like it?
3. Do you find yourself drinking/taking drugs etc. more than you would like?
4. Do you openly talk about your happiness with anyone (friend, spouse, therapist, etc.)?

While the list of questions above is not ultimately comprehensive, it should be able to give you a good first indication of whether or not you are lying to yourself about your level of happiness. Remember this quote if you are unsure how important it is, to be honest with yourself:

"Above all, don't lie to yourself. The man who lies to himself and listens to his own lie comes to a point that he cannot distinguish the truth within him, or around him, and so loses all respect for himself and for others." - Fyodor Dostoevsky (Russian novelist and philosopher).

Should We Even Pursue Happiness

There is a famous saying that has been popularized for being the embodiment of the United State of America and its life philosophy which goes as follows:

"Life, liberty and the pursuit of happiness".

The pursuit of happiness is one that is deeply embodied by humans all across the world and has inspired many works of fiction (take for example *The Pursuit of Happiness, 2006,* which stars Will Smith). However, if you remember the points made earlier in this book you may remember that many people go astray when pursuing happiness and end up in a place which is detrimental to them and those around them. This can leave one begging the question: should we even pursue happiness?

The answer, as it often is, seems to be nuanced. While the pursuit of happiness should be incorporated into everybody's life, as it must be for you if you are reading this book, it should not take the center stage in terms of your priorities. The answer cannot be simple because human beings are complex and find themselves in many different situations. As stated previously, a large amount of the population is depressed, and one aspect of depression is a severe lack of joy in general experiences. In a case such as this, it would be simple to say that it would be beneficial to pursue happiness. At the same time remembering that happiness isn't something that we PURSUE Out There, in the world but something that we DEVELOP within ourselves.

The key to knowing whether or not you should pursue happiness depends on the methodology you would want to implore in order to achieve your desire. For example, if you have a light sense of depression and believe that if you would just take a little bit of ecstasy once in a while in order to counteract the problem, your methodology is flawed from the start. However, if you decide that you would combat the problem initially by eating more nutrient-dense foods and beginning an exercise routine then you are on the right track. When deciding on methodology your focus should be long-term happiness and not short-term happiness or more aptly put, gratification.

When one does take into account this point then the answer becomes clearer: if you are dissatisfied with your life then you should pursue happiness to a certain degree. However, it is also important to place your focus upon long-term happiness and to choose a methodology that is beneficial to those around you as well to a certain extent. We will cover this more in part three. However, if you feel content with your life then you do not necessarily need to continue your pursuit of happiness at all. As the saying goes 'don't fix what isn't broken'.

Is Happiness the Only Thing That Matters?

In short, the answer is simple: no. There are many things in this life that should be valued equally with happiness and we as humans know this intrinsically. This is why we believe it to be noble to suffer for the sake of something greater. You may not be happy for example when you are doing your 2-hour daily cardio session while you are preparing for military deployment, and when you do finally get deployed you may witness terrible acts of violence, but you endure these things because you are working towards something that is more important than your happiness.

For most people, purpose supersedes happiness (as mentioned in the example above) but there are plenty of other things that people also value more than happiness including their faith, family, or friends. It is good to remind yourself of the position, in terms of priorities, that happiness takes in your overall life. But remember that it is not the only thing that matters.

Is Struggle Essential for Happiness?

As mentioned above struggle often means that we are not happy. You cannot really be happy and truly struggle at the same time. However, what about the struggle for the sake of obtaining happiness? That is a slightly different story. The struggle is an undeniable part of the human experience. And while they are undoubtedly uncomfortable, they are necessary in order for us to learn and grow as people according to Life Labs Psychologies (2018). Without struggle, it is almost impossible to become the best version of yourself and so it should be embraced rather than avoided.

However, it has to also be said that the kind of struggle is very important. There are positive and negative stressors in life. A positive stressor is one that will create growth in the person undergoing it. A negative stressor on the other hand will cause a person to break down. Think of the difference between lifting weights for gaining muscle and being beaten up by a gang of drunken teenagers. While both experiences may be painful, the former is positive stress because it is controlled and designed for growth. Therefore, when one looks at whether or not you have to struggle to be happy the question could be extended to: do you need to struggle to obtain anything good in life?

The answer, for the vast majority of people, will be yes. However, there are those who can achieve it without much struggle. These people are outliers and should not be used as an example of how the average person can achieve happiness.

Do You Value Happiness?

We spoke earlier at length about the importance of being honest with yourself and there is one question you should definitely ask yourself: do you truly value happiness? The reason it is so important to pose this question to yourself is that most people, while they may say that they want to be happy, do not value it as much as they should. Often times these people will engage in behavior that makes them unhappy, whether it be staying in a job that they hate or not allowing themselves to eat dessert once in a while even though they are perfectly healthy.

Psychology Today (2014) refers to this phenomenon as self-punishment. The act of making yourself miserable. However, they also state that the act can be beneficial as people use it for mild motivation when necessary. However, there is a very unhealthy form of self-punishment in which the person practicing it is trying to atone for unresolved guilt which they may be harboring from a difficult experience. They may have cheated on their spouse or claimed someone else's work as their own. Whatever the guilt-inducing stimulus is, if left undealt with, many people will resort to self-punishment as a way to alleviate the feeling of guilt. Unfortunately, in many cases, the guilt does not dissipate and the cycle of self-punishment becomes normative, moving from a conscious decision to a subconscious act.

When it has occurred, the people suffering may have lost sight of their value for happiness. However, by once again examining whether or not happiness is important to you it is possible to negate the negative side-effects of self-punishment. Because once you start to realize that happiness should be important, especially your own, then it is more likely that you will take the type of actions that will result in you living a happier life and acting to increase your happiness.

How Does Someone Attain Lasting Joy and Happiness In 2020 and Into the Future?

This is a difficult question to answer, and more details will be provided in the latter part of this book, but for now, there are some things that you can do in order to obtain happiness.

1. Health Optimization

It is no coincidence that in the common saying 'health, wealth and happiness' the first of the trio is health. Poor health choices, such as excessive smoking, drinking, and bad dietary choices are responsible for decreased numbers of neurotransmitters, such as serotonin and dopamine, without which it is going to be difficult to experience much happiness (NCBI, 2008). It is also common sense that if you are sick a lot or are suffering from a chronic illness, that it is going to be far more difficult to enjoy life because of the physical restrictions that entail. So, if you want to increase your happiness then you should work to improve your health. Simple ways to do this is to eat healthier, drink more water, engage in some exercise, and go to bed earlier to increase the amount of sleep you get. All of these things will have long-term health benefits that will ultimately increase your happiness.

2. Pursuing Your Dreams

Far too many people are told that their dreams will never come true and that they should stick to their day-jobs. And to a certain extent this may be true, it is important not to throw away your financial security. However, in 2020 it is easier than ever before to not give up on your personal passions, despite any other work you may be doing. By beginning to do some work in an area you love while you are still working your normal job you will be able to slowly see more and more opportunities to gain finances through that particular area and eventually you will be able to transition to doing it full-time. And so, do not let other people discourage you from achieving this, there are millions of people who are happy today because they are pursuing their dreams and passions. Again, The Better Life Experience program may help.

3. Focus on Relationships

When it comes to measuring happiness, science has helped us to find one of the most important aspects of life, relationships. The Independent (2017) reported on research done to determine what makes people the happiest in the world, and the results were undoubtedly in the favor of close relationships. Therefore, if you find yourself to be a bit of a loner, it may be worthwhile to go out and socialize more to obtain closer friendships as a way to increase your happiness. Likewise, if there is a lot of stress in the close relationships that you do have it may be worth seeking counseling or other forms of reconciliation to boost your level of happiness.

Is It Ever Too Late to Find Happiness?

In a world surrounded by pessimism, it may be hard to believe that happiness is possible. Unfortunately, as people age, they tend to become more rigid in their viewpoints of the world, including their ability to find happiness. However, whether you are 80 or 18 the same thing rings true, it is not too late for you to obtain happiness. The ability to do so is right there at your fingertips and is not dependent on your financial situation, connections, or any other things immediately outside of your control. All it requires is the desire for improvement and change and then implementing small steps every single day.

What Is Your Current Real Source of Happiness?

To begin your personal happiness journey, it may be beneficial for you to start with a positive and identify where your current source of happiness lies. It may be that you have a really fruitful and engaging marriage which makes you look forward to coming home each day. Or on the other hand, you may have just started a new career path that excites you. Whatever your personal source of happiness currently is, it is important to identify for two reasons.

The first is because you do not want to place your focus on something which does not require any work. If you are happy in your marriage then do not waste time going to therapy in order to obtain even greater levels of happiness from it. Likewise, if you love your job, do not begin to spend more time at work in order to maximize your happiness. Taking this course of action will likely lead to a decline in happiness over time as a balance needs to be a core aspect of everything that makes you happy.

The second reason is motivation. It may be that you feel like your life is severely lacking happiness. However, even people who suffer from depression often have a few things that bring them joy. Identifying these things and making yourself aware that you can experience happiness will help to give you the internal energy required to seek after more.

Is Happiness A Choice

Many people will not like to hear the answer to this question, but nonetheless, it is important to know. Happiness, to a certain extent, is a choice that you can make. There is a concept in psychology known as 'victim mentality'. When someone is caught up in this mind space it usually causes them to shift blame and responsibility to everyone and everything apart from themselves. You may have engaged with many people who are stuck in this thinking pattern, or it may have even been you who is guilty of this. They are easy to identify by the amount they complain about things and people, rather than talking about their own short-comings.

Unfortunately, this mentality has seeped into people's way of thinking when it comes to happiness. 'I am miserable because of my wife' or 'How can I be happy when my boss constantly treats me like this' maybe some of the common phrases of someone stuck in a victim mentality. The key point is actually that oftentimes their complaints are justified. It really does become largely more difficult to be happy if you are surrounded by negative or stressful people or circumstances. However, more difficult and impossible are not the same thing. When you realize that you have some control, however, minute it may be, you begin to give yourself the power to change.

Take for example an overweight individual. It may have been that they were often mistreated at work and therefore resorted to overeating as a way to comfort themselves. After a few years of repeating this pattern they say "It is not my fault that I am overweight, it is the people who mistreated me that are to blame!" What this person is saying is technically true, but they are also shifting all of the responsibility rather than just some to other people, starving themselves of the power to change. However, if the person would have said "because of the people that mistreated me, it is going to be extremely difficult for me to lose weight, but I can still do it" they have allowed themselves to gain personal power over their situation while at the same time still rightfully acknowledging the fault of others in their situation. Therefore happiness, just like so many other things in life, is a choice that you can make. And indeed claim!

What Is Wrong with Making Everyone Happy First?

Have you ever heard of the saying: you can't give what you do not have? Nowhere is this truer than with happiness. People often try to obtain happiness by making other people happy, even though they are themselves miserable. This is a plan that is destined for failure. If you truly want to make those around you happier, and as functional adults this is something you may want to strive towards, the true way of achieving the goal is by focusing on your own happiness instead. People are drawn to those who are happy, and if you yourself are filled with happiness it will be simple for you to share it with those around you. Always make yourself happy first. The reasons for this will become much clearer in part three of this book.

Why Is Happiness the Key to Success

As mentioned, many times before in this book, happiness and success are linked, one is not truly possible without the other. Many people want to become successful. They want to get promoted, start a successful business, or have a large house with multiple garages. However, what they often fail to realize is that those things, devoid of happiness, are not worth having. Success can be seen as a measure of how happy something makes us. If a relationship makes you truly happy and joyful (from a long-term perspective) it could be seen as a success, even if other people in your life think that it is not. Likewise, a job that brings in $30,000 a year but brings you to utmost joy every day is a far greater success than earning $500,000 a year but hating your work. And if you do have big goals and ambitions, in terms of external defining factors, then you cannot neglect your own happiness first. Make yourself happy as it will give you the strength and energy you need to succeed in your endeavor's.

PART 2:

Your Three Life's

The Essential Foundation of Success,
Life and Happiness

FOUNDATION OF SUCCESS

Essential Steps to Greater Success in Life

What is it that makes some people more successful than others?

More importantly, what is it that makes some people happier than others?

Of course, you can always point to luck and you can always point to outside factors. Sure, there is often an element of knowing the right people, of being in the right place at the right time, of being born with a silver spoon in your mouth, and so on.

But if you constantly focus on the factors that are outside your control then you will never reach your full potential. Not only that, but there are also *plenty* of examples of people who have beaten the odds. People who were born into poverty, who perhaps didn't have the opportunities that others did. Of course, there are also plenty of examples of people who dropped out of school or college, and yet some of these people still managed to become immensely successful.

Likewise, you can have two people in the precise same situation but they might be completely different in terms of how happy they are and how they perceive their 'lot' in life.

The difference? Successful and happy people have the right *thought processes behind them and the right direction before them*.

The Negative Side of Positive Thinking

But having said that, there is a hidden and often overlooked danger in acting on processes that are purely *positive thinking* in nature. It is true, positive thinkers do tend to have the ability to look at a situation and see the glass as half full so to speak. They can spot some opportunities and then take those opportunities and make the most of them. But seriously, *"make the most of them"?* Real success stories don't just *"make the most of"*, a situation. They control the situations and opportunities before them.

To that end, many will tell you that *everything* starts with the right mindset, positive thinking being at the core of that mindset and although the right mindset can help you to accomplish more, and to be more effective, it isn't the first step towards greater success.

So, to say that everything first begins with the right mindset is a presumption or half-truth at best, and of course, favored by many mindset experts, promoters, and gurus with a vested interest in its promotion. But don't get me wrong, I don't want to downplay the importance of mindset. It is critical but there are also other considerations.

You see, when someone starts to work on their mindset, they inevitably begin to think more positively. They adopt the phrase, *"eliminate the negatives, accentuate the positives,"* and in most cases, they eliminate the negative by focusing solely on the positives until the negative isn't a part of the individual's focus.

This is delusion at best and can be dangerous to a person's success and achievements, and that doesn't lead to greater success. It leads to more of the same whether you feel great about it or not. But the same applies to positive thinking here. I don't want to downplay it. It is an essential part of thinking your way to success but it isn't the be-all and end-all of success. In fact, it should be taken as a given and not an option one must adopt as if joining an elite cult of some kind.

Positive thinking does not change the environment around you, it changes your perception of it and in most cases to the detriment of the success of seeking individual. Although, long term it can make a difference, and as suggested it is an important part of thinking your way into a better life experience.

Essentially, the right mindset is only the fifth step in the success building process at best. The first, second, and third steps, along with the vital importance of gaining greater happiness are usually completely bypassed and so we will discuss them briefly in the following pages.

So now the only remaining question is, "What are the steps to greater success?" ...from wherever you find yourself now!

Well, that is, of course, the subject of this section which is, if you will, a guide that helps you take the first few steps followed by the possibility of taking many more of the steps only alluded to in the phrase, "the journey of a thousand miles begins with the first step".

So, let's discover these first crucial steps together.

Your Three Life's - Essential Foundations

When you decide for yourself to travel down the road to greater success, the first thing you must absolutely understand and get clear on is the fact that you have three lives and not just the one.

We will discuss **Your Three Life's** briefly below to give you an idea of this concept and how to best create a better life and *a better life experience* for you and those you care about in your life.

Your First Life: Your External Life

In broad terms, your external life can be easily summed up by What You DO, or your ACTIONS. Of course, your actions will be determined by YOUR PURPOSE and Creative Life.

Your External Life or Actions are also closely related to your Internal Life or your Mindset. In fact, everything that you do in your outer life is colored by your Internal Life or Mindset.

What you do becomes more enjoyable and mostly improved as your Inner State or Mindset improves. You could say that **Your Actions Are an Effect of Your Thoughts**. But the results you attain from your actions are **not** determined by your thoughts alone! In that case, Reality is the teacher. Or Your EXPERIENCES!

It is traditional that the external part of your life should become occupied by a job or career, a relationship, friendships, and usually but not always, a hobby or interest. Remember here we are just generalizing and not dividing your life into sections or blocks. We are speaking of what is usually true for everyone or at the very least, most people.

By definition, knowing your purpose then leads to a Primary Aim or Primary Goal. Therefore, Your Actions would be best served by pursuing Your PURPOSE Through a set of **Clearly Defined Projects & Goals.**

It goes without saying that what you do with your life determines the results that you get. But it is also commonplace to:

1. Educate and improve yourself.
2. Find yourself in good employment.
3. Earn your way to a good career.

Then everything that you do, including health and relationships usually fits around those three focal points if you are moderately ambitious. At the same time saving as much money as possible in order to live an even better life one day. With greater happiness within it and as a result.

This is just a simple yet most likely accurate view of Your External

Life and you most likely fit into one part or another and on the scale somewhere between rich and poor, success and failure, and so on. Most fit into this scale around the mediocrity mark.

Your Second Life: Your Inner Life

Your Inner Life eludes somewhat to mindset, but in this instance, mindset is more of an effect and although it is mentioned here, the fifth step of mindset integrates with your inner life that we are describing here.

Your inner life is concerned with anything and everything that is within you. It is true that mindset colors everything in your life, but in the process of creating *a better life experience*, mindset is still only the fifth step in the process. But as suggested from that fifth step or level, it integrates with everything else in your life and with each step as we will soon discover.

Why is that? Well, it's simple, I speak of three life's but this again alludes to the fact that you are a whole being and have just one life. The division into three lives is then an analogy to help the individual understand each part of the one life they have more fully. The individual can then act to improve one or all areas in order to create an even better version of himself or herself and thus have *a better life experience*. This is covered in more detail as well as the implications of your three life's in the online program version.

So, let's go on... your inner life can be divided into various parts such as emotions, state of mind, thoughts, reactions, senses, etc. However, in more general terms your inner life is composed of just two distinct parts. Your THOUGHTS and Your EMOTIONS collectively called your STATE of MIND/being. Or as is more commonplace in today's world... Your Mind State or MINDSET.

Remember this is just a generalization.

Developing the appropriate Mindset or in this case, your inner attributes that support your Actions and your PURPOSE is an absolutely vital part of all success.

Your Third Life: Your Creative Life

As with the other two life's your creative life (personal hobby, interest, or business life) can theoretically be divided into many sections or blocks, but in more general terms we are speaking here of **What You Create or What You CHOOSE for yourself.**

Whether that's creating a painting or a business. Or whatever your personal interests and passions in life just happen to be.

And again, what you create is usually an effect of your two other lives and the experiences you have within those two lives'. Or more aptly put, what you create is usually a self-determined pursuit based on your thought's feelings, past actions, and experiences. These are then directed towards a given end, pursuit, or interest.

However, in this instance, we are speaking of what you create in order to eliminate the traditional, job-based, external life as well as achieve the ideal internal life in order to have a much better and forever expanding EXPERIENCE.

A SINGLE and BETTER LIFE... What we term your "E" Life or "eLife". Or, YOUR LIFE PURPOSE!

So, that you can eventually *Master Your Destiny.*

Your Integrated Life

Your three life's can be moved around into any, or no particular order that suits you. You can place your first life, second or third and your second life first or third, and so on.

However, it's important to note that to divide an individual into any number of parts in order to make sense of the whole is, in reality, a futile undertaking, simply because when such division begins other realities are constantly unearthed and often to the contrary.

For example, in our attempt to separate the OUTER from the INNER life we begin to glimpse that the two are completely integrated, much like the sense of touch isn't realized within until the external, tactile world becomes involved. The same can be said of hearing, seeing, and feeling.

Something felt within is, as far as we can tell an effect of an external occurrence or experience whether past present, or even regarding a future occurrence. We feel pain FROM the outside world (but not always) through the nervous system and into the brain. We become depressed or any number of other feeling states due to combinations of and integrations with external factors, whether past or present.

As you begin to see, there really is no inner at all, despite such phrases as "search within for the answer", "concentrate within" etc. WITHIN is the culmination of the effects of and integration with the EXTERNAL.

So, how can we use this to achieve greater success in life?

Three Steps to Succeeding at Anything

What follows is an abridged version of the whole philosophy of your three life's which integrates with what I call The Primary Concept as explained within The Better Life Experience program, mentioned at the back of this book.

The Better Life experience program deals with the first step in this process.

Step 1: Know What You Want!

The first step of knowing what you want is easier said than done. Knowing what you want is really finding or choosing a purpose for your life or life purpose.

Step 2: Knowing How to Get Where You Want

Of course, once you know what you want the question becomes how do I get there? This is then really a two-level process. But for now, let's just say it's a single process of setting the goals that will lead you to what you want.

Well, that sounds simple enough but, it isn't quite that simple, especially if you want to achieve massive things in life. And who doesn't, right? I digress...

Step 3: How to Get What You Want

Of course, setting appropriate goals and creating appropriate plans to get you where you want to be in life is essential if you want to succeed at anything, and that question was answered in the previous step. But then why is this step titled How to Get What You Want? Surely that's just a repeat of step two?

Well no, in step two the "How" was how you move from where you are to where you want to be or the actions you take, and we discovered that the way to do that is through setting goals, large or small, depending on what you decided that you wanted to experience in your life in step 1.

This next step deals with "How" or "Who" you are being to get there, but mostly "How" you become who you need to be that will enable you to get Where You Want to Be and therefore Get What You Want.

This is really the true domain of the *mindset* of how you think, act, and behave as you move towards what you want. But mindset becomes the fifth step in this illustration. Step three was just an explanation of it.

Responsibility

Although in the three-step process above we said that:

1.   The first step is to: Know What You Want.
2.   The second step is to: Know How You Are Going to Get There.
3.   And the third step is to: Know HOW you are going to make the journey. Who you are being and so on?

The truth is that the above steps are really steps, two, three, and four.

The real, first, and most important step is simply to learn to take responsibility for your own actions, your mental state, and more importantly, your circumstances which include your level of happiness. Undertaking the journey into and towards success in a miserable unhappy negative state or even a mildly positive state will only produce mildly positive results at best.

So, you must first accept that the situation you are in right now is because of you and that *you* have the power to change it. Only you can change what you have created and continue to create more of and so create something new.

The problem is that many people assume that their situation is largely dictated by outside factors. They then begin to blame their circumstances on luck or even on other people.

- You don't have the job you want because you didn't have the luxury to look around when you first left

school, college, or university.
- You can't go traveling because you have a family.
- You aren't rich because you were born in the wrong generation, in the wrong part of town...

...and so on.

There may be some truth to these things sure, but it is also up to you to dig yourself out of that situation and that's something that we've already seen is possible. Do you think that Richard Branson made these kinds of excuses? Or Steve Jobs? Or the thousands of others that gravitated to great heights?

If you don't take responsibility for your actions, then you can't be expected to achieve all the things you want to achieve because you'll just find an external reason to lay the blame at. You need to believe that you have an impact on your life and you need to have an understanding of Your Three Life's to gain more focus and then control. As suggested the online version of Your Three Lives adds another dimension to the whole process.

An Additional Integrating Step
So, the three steps are really all that is required to begin moving closer to greater success. But there are two additional steps as previously suggested. The fourth foundational and integrated step to even greater success no matter where you find yourself now is to analyze your current life in every area. You must **Eliminate the Negatives**, NOT just bypass them, and hope that they go away. They won't.

You need to take responsibility and then ACT to create a better life experience and you do that by:

1. Knowing what you want.
2. Knowing how you are going to get there.
3. Knowing who you need to be in order to get there.

4. Eliminate the negatives that are working against you and may stop you from getting there.

5. Develop the mindset to take you beyond the negatives to where you want to be.

But the essential integrating fourth step is to **Examine your life and Eliminate the Negatives** and continue to do so as you learn about what you want, how you are going to get there, and who you are being in order to get there. So, step four is really step zero. An integrating step. This brings to mind a very important and often overlooked part of any or most step-by-step systems that you follow in your future or that you may have followed in your past. Each step integrates with each other.

So, step 4 in our previous examples is step 0, step 1, step 2, step 3, step 4, and step 5. And step 1, is also step 2, 3, 4, and 5. Each step integrates with and is directly linked to the other steps.

Eliminating the Negatives is essentially an integrating factor as we suggested. But so are each of the other steps.

Ok, so what the heck does that mean. Well, let's say you just did step 1. Sooner or later you will realize that you needed to add the other steps. Or, let's say that you started at step 2. You will soon realize that although you may have the vehicle to get you there and, in this example, the vehicle is setting goals. You don't know step 1 (what you want) and so you have to integrate that step. You will then need to integrate steps 3, 4, and 5 to be able to make the journey.

Just as your three life's is an analogy (which incidentally is why it is grammatically spelled wrong) to illustrate how the human mechanism begins to work. So too are the 3 steps or five steps. They are really just one integrated step.

Once the negatives are eliminated (in step 0), you can then focus on the positives, or what I prefer to call **Imagine the Possibilities** as you move through your life with more **purpose** and with fewer obstacles or what I refer to as the negatives. Negative behaviors, habits, circumstances, and even addictions in some cases.

Only by accepting this can you then recognize the power you have to make any change you like. Yes, with great power comes great responsibility. But you know what else? With great responsibility, comes great power! You are that power, you just need to take responsibility and begin your journey to greater success by first **Eliminating the Negatives.** All of them, one by one!

Happiness - The Key to Greater Success

When you think about the negatives in your life in both your past and your present life it should become clear that gaining more happiness is what we are all really after. It is the reason we want to remove the negatives in our life. It is the reason we want what we want and it is the reason we go through the efforts to undertake the journey.

We believe that eliminating them will afford us more happiness. We believe that when we get what we want we will be happy or happier.

But the error in this kind of thinking is that we place our happiness out there in an unknown future. We place conditions that block our happiness. Whether we want to eliminate the negatives and then we will be happy, or whether we want a new car and then we will be happy, doesn't really matter. The fact is that we block our own happiness with our desires for anything.

The thing we want is out there in the future. It must be, simply because you don't have it at present and so we create separation between us and our desires and even our own happiness.

The key then is to integrate our efforts. We must integrate our efforts to clean up our past and present life, remove the negatives as we go, and experience happiness in the present moment and not at a future time that frankly, may never happen.

Think about this for a moment... we believe that achieving more success, whether it's getting a new car, taking a much-needed holiday, achieving more success in our career, job, or business will make us happier. And the bigger the success that you want to experience the more unhappy you become and the further away your happiness is. Yet the truth is, those things will either never come or will be more difficult to manifest into our experience UNLESS WE ARE HAPPY. First!

Sadly, many have got it completely backward. Just think about it. The people we need and that have what we want don't want to be around sad, miserable, or less than joyful people, why would they? They want to be around happy people and so when you are happy, the people who can help you get where you want to be are much more obliging to our plight. Then there's the vibrational thing which is a completely different story.

If you noticed, there is another integrating factor right there. We need other people who have what we want but at the same time, we need ourselves to undergo the journey and to do the work.

So, without analyzing our past and current life we will find it very difficult to move away from it into a better life and a better life experience. We must, therefore:

- Eliminate the Negatives
- Imagine the Possibilities
- Then move through life with purpose.

And at the same time build our personal happiness as we go.

But there are good and bad ways to do that, a wrong way and a right way. That is why I created a short program to help you get over this integrated first step: Eliminating the Negatives. And beyond!

Without going through the process each succeeding step will be so much more difficult, but because your very best investment is an investment in yourself makes the Eliminate the Negatives a no-brainer. But as suggested you can go it alone if you like and I am sure you will do pretty well. But there is nothing like going through the process in a more efficient manner to get to the things that you want and indeed, to discover what you really want and then move rapidly towards that end.

The program is called: **Eliminate the Negatives - Essential Steps to Succeed at Anything!** and is available through a four-part series. Each document part will take you through a specific process and guide you with some underlying principles and concepts everyone should know.

You will find details of the 4-part program at the back of this book.

Either way, whether you decide to go it alone or move through the Eliminate the Negatives short program I wish you great success on your journey and sincerely hope that you move rapidly towards even greater success and your dream life.

PART 3:

Upgrade Your Happiness

Upgrade Your Happiness

Moving into Who You Want to Be

So, what is the whole purpose of your three life's? Well, without understanding this essential concept and the position that you are in right now can you never really move beyond it, simply because you wouldn't know what you were moving beyond and into. Without this understanding growing, progressing, or achieving anything of note would be just about impossible and limited at best. This is why first we must *Know Ourselves* and then *Know Where We Are Heading*, and you may have a vague idea about that but let's put that aside until the Second Master Step as we make preparations for that step right now, should you decide to take that step.

Now, back to happiness! Once your three life's are in place and you're constantly working to Eliminate the Negatives covered in Master Step 1 within the Your Three Life's online program... you need to then create the best possible conditions for success. You must create more happiness. It's not simply a matter of wanting happiness any more but it becomes essential that you gain more happiness for the new situation, (your vision) that will be first uncovered, defined, and clarified in the Second Master Step... to come into being into your present and to transform into your present and current NOW.

Don't worry if this sounds a little complex, it is really simple and will become much clearer after reading this whole document.

As you should begin to see by now, the moment we call now is constantly evolving into something more conducive to what you want to be, do, and have **if**, you act on those things. But let's just stick with *being* here for the sake of simplicity and clarity.

You are becoming something and someone new in every moment of now through your thoughts and beliefs, your actions and plans, and your constant refining of those beliefs and actions.

This is how your reality is changed or created. There is no other route to a more successful life with more happiness in it. So, let's get into this somewhat elusive condition called happiness.

First, it's important to understand that most people experience fleeting happiness for one reason or another and it's important to understand that this usually occurs due in most part to some outside influence, event, or experience. But true happiness is within your right now. And, much like your vision for the future you just need to choose it. You need to choose happiness.

So, let's dig a little deeper into that right now...

Two Kinds of Happiness

As suggested, there are two kinds of happiness that an individual can experience, but like many things in life, it is vital that you get that it is the second type of happiness that you should strive for, and that we are going to build within this short program. So, what are the two types of happiness?

Hedynamic Happiness

The first type of happiness is what many but not all people strive for generally. That striving is really a result of the way modern life has been structured. It's called hedynamic happiness or happiness that is the effect of an external source. And as we have discovered within the Your Three Life's section, we want to be at cause in our lives and not at effect. Effect of external stimuli such as:

- Getting drunk
- Taking drugs
- Negative addictions

Or even more positive variations of this such as:

- Someone special visiting you unannounced
- Enjoying a family day out
- A special occasion such as a birthday

Now although the positive events listed above often produce happiness, we want those events to instead enhance our real and constant happiness not replace it as the source of our only true personal happiness. That is, they become a crutch which basically gives your power to be happy away to someone or thing external to yourself in either a positive or negative way. But that's not to say that we shouldn't enjoy the positive sources of external happiness, we absolutely should. Positive external sources of happiness become a problem when those sources become a crutch that you rely on for your own and only source of happiness.

Happiness is a gift that you give to yourself ~ Andy Raingold

Hedynamic Happiness relies on external events, people, society, as well as other external sources and, are in most cases, sources of instant gratification experienced briefly for a single, brief moment. The individual who relies on hedynamic happiness then searches for external sources to make them happy instead of cultivating real lasting happiness from within.

Udynamic Happiness

The second type of happiness is called Udynamic Happiness. It is happiness within yourself and that is self-created no matter what the external social or other events that may occur in a person's life.

As we will discover, true happiness comes from within an individual and in fact, already exists within the individual but as suggested he or she must choose to feel the happiness which often gets blocked by a series of layers that need to be uncovered before the happiness can be reached on a consistent basis at will.

The Six Layers That Block Happiness

There are essentially six layers that need uncovering and dealing with in order to achieve lasting happiness.

They are:

1. Your Desires
2. Your Current Limiting Belief Systems
3. Your Individual Identity & Ego
4. Time
5. Your Current Patterns of Conditioning
6. Your Mood and Emotions.

Briefly, the first three of the six layers are related to and begin in the external world. Your desires are formed based on something in the external world so it is external circumstances and things that color your desires.

More often than not, what we desire from the external world colors our personal bias as to what true happiness means to us and what we need to achieve in order to be happy. By doing this we separate ourselves from happiness by placing a condition on what happiness is to us and what we need to be, do, or have in order to experience it.

For instance, let's say that you need the latest model of Mercedes to truly make you happy and so until the moment that you get the Mercedes you automatically believe that you won't be happy and so you are not happy. Because you don't have the Mercedes.

When you eventually get the Mercedes, the happiness you experience is only temporary and fleeting and so your state of happiness was due to an external source which of course means that it is temporary. Hedynamic Happiness.

Because we get to choose happiness, we do not really need the Mercedes in the first place to be happy. We can make that choice before we get the Mercedes and without actually owning one. Then when we do get it, we will feel a happiness boost but it won't be fleeting happiness because you were already happy before the Mercedes came along. It was just a fleeting boost which then delivers us back to our usual state of happiness.

Ironically choosing to be happy and then acting "as if" we already own the Mercedes the quicker it will materialize into our lives. In order to do that we need to redefine what happiness really means to us and to then choose it without placing a condition on it.

Something to also note is that it isn't the fact that we don't have the Mercedes that makes us unhappy at all. It is our thoughts that we don't have it that makes us unhappy, simply because we placed a condition on our happiness. We created separation.

The First Step to Happiness

As a first step to upgrading your current happiness, you absolutely must define what happiness means to you in every area of your life and you must be specific with the answers you give when you ask the following questions for each of your desires in each area of your life.

As with most things in life the first step is usually getting clear on where you are and where you want to be regarding a specific area of life or desire. Remember that the point of the Your Three Life's section is for you to gain an understanding of where you are right now and the tool you have available to improve that life and get where you want to be or move towards it at the very least.

For Every Desire, You Have, Ask yourself:

- What would happiness look like in that situation?
- What would it mean to you and your life?
- When would you specifically experience it?
- Who would you be with when you experienced it?
- What is your current experience of that specific desire?

The questions above help you get clear on who you are currently in regard to happiness within a particular life area and who you will become when you attain the happiness you seek through the specific desire. And as previously suggested, your happiness must come from within and not from an external event, a person, or achievement.

There are many benefits to internal happiness... not the least is giving yourself power over yourself and your emotions. You choose all of your emotions and you choose happiness and so don't you think it makes sense to choose it yourself and not have an external influence choose it for you?

The Benefits of Happiness

Real internal happiness can affect your life in many and surprising ways, and also has many other benefits in both yourself and your life... such as:

- Improved thinking, logical, and critical thinking processes.
- Improved productivity, concentration, and focus.
- Increased success as an effect of the previous two benefits.
- Being more sociable and relatable, likable, and even more loved by friends and family.
- Clearer communication and better relationships.

- Greater capacity to heal yourself of minor and some major conditions.

All of which help you improve your life in just about every area such as relationships, business, and career.

Beware of Impatience!
However, the impatience factor can come into play here too, but why is that, and why is impatience so destructive to ourselves and our lives. Well, it is mainly due to the fact that if we make a small change in any area of ourselves or our life, we see very little results in the immediate moment. We are not instantly gratified. And even a day or two, or a week or two after the changes we made show little evidence that they made any difference at all. But it's important to realize the benefit of small changes that will eventually reap greater and greater rewards and benefits. In short, your efforts compound over time.

An Example of Impatience
Imagine if you will, a plane taking off at Heathrow Airport. The pilot begins by pointing the plane towards his destination, the Bahamas to the exact degree.

The relevant factor between point A: *Heathrow Airport* and point B: *The Bahamas* is *time* and of course *distance,* but considering only time, we see that if the pilot were just one degree off course at the beginning of the journey... Point A. He would end up hundreds of miles off course when he had traveled the distance between A and B... say 4000 miles, or viewed as time, say 8 hours flight time. He would be hundreds of miles from the Bahamas.

But that was the effect of a small change at the beginning of the journey. So, what if he made several small changes? What if the pilot started off several degrees off course at point A? Well, he would be thousands of miles away from the Bahamas once he had traveled the 4000 miles or 8 hours flight time.

So, in this analogy, you see that small changes make a massive difference to your destination and so isn't it a good choice to put impatience aside, have faith in yourself and your ability to transform yourself and your life into something more congruent with what you want to experience, and then make the effort to make the necessary changes, and then stick to them?

I think so too!

You are in effect the pilot of and to your own destination and you can make a number of small changes that help you move through your personal journey towards a greater version of who you are being and so affect the results that that new person is capable of achieving.

We covered that analogy or journey from A to B, past to present, etc. in the Main Your Three Life's documents. And as suggested in those documents you are on a journey of becoming your future self constantly, yet will always be moving in a wave between the past, present, and future points. Your future self and the self you are right now. That is how life works. That is how the human mechanism works, it is goal-oriented by nature which is why you have to eliminate the negatives and then imagine the possibilities available to you and then make the small changes to create greater outcomes and results.

The Primary Happiness & Success Blocker

Many things can separate us from our success and happiness but one of the most stubborn and destructive blockers is the addiction and adherence to our own life dramas. Negative dramas are more addictive than most drugs as they release the endorphins that create euphoria in our minds so we create more and more of those oh so sad destructive negative dramas that we believe and accept as being good and bringing happiness.

This is a vital point to understand and is the foremost reason why I developed the eliminate the negatives program which is the First Master Step after these beginning preparations. Eliminating the Negatives gives you the mind space, or vacuum to create more happiness and a better life experience. A better now.

Of course, the dramas we create and experience cause only negative emotions and patterns within us that often bring comfort and in many cases sympathy from others. We become addicted to this self-accepted, self-fulfilling prophecy that we accept and create for ourselves. It's a little comfort zone that we come to accept as being good for us when it is a silent monster slowly draining your life and trying to destroy you and your future happiness. But of course, you have to make the decision to slay the monster. There is nothing comfortable about it until you do it.

And of course, when we accept our self-created prison in this way, we find people who are quite willing to help us to enjoy our misery through connecting with us and supporting our personal drama of one kind or another. Misery does love company?

Connecting with others in this way is obviously bad for our lives and ourselves and so we must redefine what connecting to others means to us personally. How you connect and who you connect to and so on. Put another way your most dominant emotions of negativity caused by your drama become an addictive state that you hold onto and forever reinforce.

Your Automatic Targeting System

We reinforce those negative emotions and experiences through the reticular activating system which is a function of the brain that is used for goals and goal-oriented thinking. This is your personal law of attraction attractor mechanism in that what you focus on, you see more of.

Most people have experienced this at fleeting moments and called it coincidence but what was really happening was that the R.A.S was bringing your attention to a particular thing, object, or experience because you expressed a desire for that thing.

To illustrate, I am a lover of motorcycles and before I purchased my latest motorcycle all I knew about this particular model of motorcycles was that they are usually green and black. Kawasaki motorcycles are mostly dominantly green as that is part of the Kawasaki branding.

Now, when I saw one of these green and black motorcycles at a good price, I called the dealer who said, "sorry, we only have black and orange in stock", "Agh" was my response. But I told the dealer that if he sent me a video of it, I may consider buying it. To cut a long story short, he sent me a video and I fell in love with the bike.

It was black with orange and white decals and looked pretty great. So, I bought it, and a few days later it was delivered to my home.

From that point onwards I have seen approximately 6 orange and black Kawasaki's riding past me in my local village and I later joined a Kawasaki group online and there were many people who proudly posted pictures of their orange and black Kawasaki. The point is, that because I was focused on an orange and black Kawasaki of my own. I began to see them everywhere, and in effect, I was experiencing an hedynamic happiness boost. The R.A.S then brought more of those bikes into my experience such as through the online group which I would never have joined in normal circumstances.

So, when you change your focus on yourself or your goal you begin to see and experience more of it. This may be subtle at first but the closer you get to the goal, the Kawasaki in my example, the more you see of it. In other words, the more negative drama you focus on the more you see of it. The more negative emotions you accept, and the more you experience them within yourself and within your environment, the more you get of them.

As humans, we are goal-oriented by nature. Just think about it, at every moment in time you are heading somewhere, doing something, chasing down a specific outcome whether it's the goal of creating an evening meal or creating a successful online business. It matters not, you will create and experience more of it whenever it is your focus.

Are You Reacting?

Based on what we have discussed so far it should be apparent that if you are experiencing momentary feelings of joy then something is triggering your happiness and those feelings. Which as we have discovered is a hedynamic source of happiness. It's an external source.

Knowing this helps us to begin the process to pinpoint exactly what is triggering those feelings of happiness?

It is a good idea to begin a notebook and write down anything that may trigger your happiness from the outside world. If you have a good think about your life and situations that you come up against on a regular basis you should be able to discover some of those triggers right now and then write them down. Only by knowing what negative situations bring you moments of fleeting happiness or joy can you begin to change them or remove them altogether.

After you have completed this exercise you can begin the process of writing a whole bunch of good, healthy, and positive activities and things that make you feel happy and give you a boost. Although these two are external sources of happiness, it is you who is choosing them. You are taking an active part in choosing and using these external sources so they will still benefit you in the long run as you begin to build happiness from within and then use these external sources as momentary happiness boosters as and when you like.

Assessing Your Real Condition

Of course, none of what we have discussed so far will do you any good at all if you don't believe you can be happy most of the time. Or if you don't believe that you can really achieve anything in life of note.

It is actually an impossibility for an individual to not create good things by performing good productive actions. It is only negative actions that cause negative reactions and neutral actions that keep things the way they are. So, in every moment of now choose what is good for you. Choose beliefs that are good for you and choose what you want to be, do, and have.

You have one major tool going for you that will run alongside your R.A.S or personal attraction mechanism. That is your ability to imagine the possibilities available to you in this life and the life you decide and choose to create for yourself. The Eliminate the Negatives program goes into that much deeper in Master Step 1 so I won't cover it again here as it takes a whole book to describe the process and benefits of imagining the possibilities available to you.

But as you do imagine what you could achieve there are a couple of things you should make note of.

1. Do not judge yourself based on what someone else has done. If you do, you will always find a way to make yourself incapable of achieving what you want and more. It is just not true. Use your own judgment to judge your abilities and then keep your focus on what you are capable of according to your own perspectives and not your perspective of someone else's ability.

2. Cultivate the belief that you are experiencing it now.
    This involves eliminating the negatives and self-doubt.
    Believe you can and you can. Believe you can't and you
    can't. You are a self-fulfilling prophecy

    for good or bad. What do you choose?

This all clearly illustrates that who you are becoming is far more important than who you are. That is, if you want to change, grow, and improve yourself and your life. Ask yourself, who am I becoming? What am I choosing? Then choose something that helps you become who you want to become! Then act in a way that the you that you want to become would!

Releasing Your Inner Joy

So how do we uncover and upgrade your inner happiness and joy?

Well, it is quite simple... we need to systematically uncover the layers that block you from achieving happiness by calling it forth at will.

If you remember the six layers are:

7. Your Desires
8. Your Current Limiting Belief Systems
9. Your Individual Identity & Ego
10. Time
11. Your Current Patterns of Conditioning
12. Your Mood and Emotions.

Let's uncover their meanings one layer at a time...

Layer 1: What Do You Really Desire?

We have already covered desire but it will serve us to bring it up again and learn more about our own personal desires. You can begin by creating a list of all of your life categories that are important to you such as health, fitness, diet, material things, relationships, career, job, business, personal growth, finance, environment, fun, and so on. Create your own personal list of life categories. Remember though that as you grow so will your life categories change to fit your new situation. For now, choose the areas of life that are important to you right now. Include any hobby or special interest areas you have if you have them.

When you have done that make a list of the desires that you have for each life area or category. This will begin to look like a goals list but it is really about future and present desires and not goals at this point.

As you go through this process it is important to understand that some desires will be formed and accepted by yourself according to external influences and society. For instance, society has laid out a life plan for everyone that goes something like this:

- Go to school and learn.
- Leave school and get a job.
- Change jobs as needs be.
- Build a career in one area if you are able.
- Get married.
- Buy a house.
- Save.
- Retire
- Die.

Well, that list of desires is depressing, to say the least, so choose your own desires and forget about what society wants from you.

These desires are what most people follow because their parents went the same route or because of friends that are going through the same thing or and a number of external stimuli. Remove those by imagining they have no power over you and create desires of your own. You don't have to play by the same rules as everyone else.

Often, we believe that we should choose these desires because society has called these steps to success. That is what they call going through these desires. But what is success to you? What do you really desire? Often these desires will cause conflict within yourself as although you believe you should pursue a job or a career, you are more interested in starting your own business for instance.

You may experience conflict in any area related to your own true desires so make note of these conflicts of interest from your own perspectives, not someone else.

Manipulative Advertisers and Marketers
Many companies use advertising in very manipulative ways to get you to desire something that you may have absolutely no interest in desiring... yet you get influenced by these advertisers and may even fall prey to what they are attempting to push onto you. Advertising is a form of persuasion and so you need to recognize when you are being persuaded to do something against your own will and your own desires.

You must choose your happiness yourself based on your own desires and control of those desires. When you have chosen what you desire you need to then write down why you desire it. It then becomes much easier to move into a space where you are not influenced by the bombardment of ongoing persuasive media noise that removes your desires and replaces them with external desires you don't actually want.

Billions of dollars are being invested in getting you to choose something you do not want. So, the best thing to do is to create a desire diary and get clear on what you want and why you want it. How will it make you feel and so on? Get clear on all of those things for each area of your life desires in each of your personal life categories and you will have taken the first step to greater happiness and joy in your life.

You will often find that owning a specific thing will only give fleeting happiness at best so imagine what it would be like to actually own the item now and then examine your feelings. You will come to notice that you are experiencing the feelings right now and so you don't need the item in order to be happy. Choose the feeling of being happy now despite not having the item. You can do this by imagining you have the item whatever it is.

This is made possible because the brain produces happiness endorphins and distributes them through your body whether you have the item or not. It does this because it doesn't know the difference between having something that causes you to be happy or imagining yourself as having the thing you want and being happy.

This is why belief is so powerful. When you believe something to be true you imagine it as being a fact, then the brain produces the feeling of achieving the thing you believe and the R.A.S then gets you to experience more of that thing which in turn produces more feelings of happiness and this goes on as either a growth cycle or a death cycle. You are really a self-fulfilling prophecy so chose something you want to experience and not just something you can put up with. Don't put up with anything, create fulfillment within yourself and your life.

Choose to Smile
You can also choose to smile and that will bring on the feelings of happiness because the brain doesn't know the difference

between a true smile and a fake smile. So fake smile your way into experiencing more happiness beginning right now. Then after you have faked it for a while you will most likely make it, and you no doubt know the famous success axiom - *fake it till you make it.*

In other words, positive actions produce positive results. Or, like attracts like and the other self-fulfilling prophecy type axioms.

The point to all of this is simply the fact that whatever you want to be, do, or have in life is because you believe it will make you happier and give you feelings of happiness. It is the feeling that we are striving to achieve because we think we will feel better when we have achieved a particular and specific desire.

But as mentioned earlier, you don't need the thing to bring you happiness because the feeling of happiness is already within yourself, and what's more important is that you can choose it at any time. But because we have placed condition on what we need to be, do, or have in our lives in order to be happy we separate ourselves from happiness and as we have suggested, this all becomes a self-fulfilling prophecy. We are then not happy at all because we don't have the thing we desire to be, do, or have.

This can all be done through a simple process as stated below for each of your life areas.

1. Begin by defining what it is that you want.
2. Ask yourself what you want it for. What feelings are you trying to achieve?
3. Imagine that you already have the thing you desire and note the associated feelings. Are you excited, happy, enthusiastic, or any other emotional state when you imagine having the thing that you want?
4. Write down the feelings that you have associated with owning the item, desire, experience, or thing.
5. Do this for all of your desires.

6.   Ask the question, which feelings come up again and
      again. What is the emotion that comes up multiple
      times through your list of desires and emotions?

Once you have discovered what states or emotions you want to
experience you can start to experience them now by imagining
that you have the thing that is associated with the desire.

Give Yourself the Gift of Happiness

You can simply give yourself the gift of happiness at any time by
simply imagining the desire and then imagining that you already
have the desire that you want to have, do, be, or experience.
Embrace the feelings when you imagine owning the desire and
your brain will begin to give you more of those feelings by creating
experiences that produce the emotion that you want to have. And
yes, you may also get your actual desire to show up much faster
this way too.

In all of this, you remove the condition that you have placed on
your happiness and instead claim your happiness in the present
moment. You don't have to wait because you can create the
emotions that you want to experience right now.

So, begin to choose happiness in every moment as you uncover
more layers that may be blocking you from achieving the joy that
you desire.

And please don't see this as a chore. This is going to lead you into
a greater experience of happiness and so get excited about it. Feel
excited and go through each process knowing that your already
changing happiness is only going to grow and expand into your
entire world. Happiness is an infectious **ease**. No DIS!

Layer 2: What Is Really Stopping You?

As we move through our days and lives, we are constantly creating and recreating what is true for us.

We do this through conscious thinking and effort as well as our underlying unconscious beliefs. And although some beliefs serve our best interests and keep us from danger, some beliefs block our success and limit our progress as we move through life hopefully towards greater success and happiness.

For instance, you may want to become a successful business person but you believe that you don't deserve to have the wealth associated with business success. Or you may believe that you are not capable of achieving the level of success that you want. You may have a scarcity belief that stops you from ever achieving the abundance you want in your life regarding money or other life experiences. These are just a few examples but I am sure you get the picture.

In relationships, you may believe that you don't deserve to be loved, or you're not worthy of being loved or even worthy of achieving happiness, and so on.

All of these types of beliefs limit your success in each area of your life as you unconsciously filter your life through these beliefs... and so it is important to find out what these beliefs are in each area of life that you are interested in improving and succeeding within. Especially the areas in which you may find yourself limited no matter how hard you try to succeed in that area.

The first step to uncovering your limiting beliefs is to discover what they are. I go into this in more detail within the Eliminate the Negatives Program so I will more concisely touch upon it here.

To get started follow this simple process.

1. Make a list of each of your life categories or areas of interest to you.
2. Then make a list of things that may be holding you back such as things that you think, have learned about that area, or say to yourself regarding this area... I don't deserve to do this, whatever it is... I can't do this or I will never be able to do this and so on. Think deeply about this to discover what you really believe about each particular area of your life.
    a. Include everything that you can recall or what other people have said in the past or are currently saying about this area of life and about your own abilities and so on.
    b. Think back when you were young to what your parents and elders may have said was true or what you should or must do in this area.

Once you have your list of limiting beliefs such as in financial matters... you might believe some or all of the following beliefs:

- Money doesn't grow on trees
- Who do you think I am Rothschild/Rockefeller?
- Money is hard to get
- You have to work hard
- You will never be rich
- You can't handle that
- Rich people are mean
- You have to be mean and nasty to be rich
- Only mean, nasty people, become rich
- I wasn't born at the right time

Or in happiness you may believe:

- I don't deserve to be happy
- I will never be happy
- I haven't got time to be happy

- I wasn't meant to be happy
- Other people are happy but I can never be happy

And so on…

Whatever you believe to be true in each area of your life will become true because you are a self-fulfilling prophecy as we have mentioned previously and through the R.A.S you will create more of what you believe you are capable of. More of what you focus on consciously as well as unconsciously.

Once you have created your list of limiting beliefs it's time to turn them around but before you do that it's important to note that by being aware of a limiting belief you have neutralized it and have already begun to change. But then if you do nothing about it the belief will begin to grow again in the same direction. That's why it's vital that you create new beliefs through affirmations.

For instance, if you believe that money doesn't grow on trees, therefore it is hard to find and create in your own life, you would simply make an affirmation of the opposite kind. So, if you believe that money doesn't grow on trees then you should create an affirmation that supports your success such as, "money grows from the values I create and provide to others". And then create supporting beliefs such as, "money is abundant in my life", "I have an abundance of money", and so on.

As you begin to use your new affirmations, these new beliefs will begin to override your current limiting beliefs and then eventually become unconscious.

But how long will this take?

They say that a bad habit or belief takes approximately 21 days to become embedded subconsciously but I have found that it takes approximately 31 days. You may find it takes 61 days until your new beliefs begin to take hold but don't let that discourage you. Create your affirmations and use them morning noon and night for 31, 61, 91, or 1001 days until you thoroughly believe that you deserve the things that you want or whatever your affirmation is supposed to be.

An important thing to note is to not beat yourself up if you miss an afternoon affirmation session, or slack off a little in the evening. So long as you pursue them first thing in the morning you should start to see results in no time at all. Again, I go into this in much more detail in the Eliminate the Negatives Program so make sure that you begin here then go deeper into all of this through that program and beyond. Remember all of this is a process of growth and we all know that plants need constant watering and feeding in order to produce the flowers or harvest.

And don't forget to change general beliefs such as the ones most people are brought up believing. "life is hard", or "life is what you make it". Instead affirm, "life is easy and supports my dreams and desires" or similar, and "I make my life a series of joyous events", or something similar. Don't be afraid to personalize my simple suggestions, by the way, that way they become much more powerful and personalized for you.

There's another belief many take up that goes, "good things come to those who wait." That is the same as separating you from happiness and basically states that if you want to be happy and have good things in your life then you will have to wait for them. Those so-called words of wisdom are more like words of folly and manipulation. Instead, affirm "good things come to me constantly and on a daily basis," or similar.

I have a personal favorite in this regard. It was found on Andrew Carnegie's desk after his death. It read "All is well and getting better, everything will turn out just so".

This can be a fun process so don't make it a chore that you just get through. Reflect on your life in each area past and present to come up with what you truly believe in each area. You can then begin the process to eliminate them and create a better more joyous life for yourself and your loved ones.

Remember too, that as you complete this step and begin your new affirmative life that you discover other beliefs that pop into your head at times when you are not expecting them to. Make note of these and work on them too. The conscious mind can become so active that it blocks the unconscious memories from surfacing but when you decide to take a walk or jump into the shower your unconscious begins to throw out ideas and past situations that rooted a particular negative belief.

Layer 3: Who Are You?

In simple terms, your personal identity is created from your past experiences. That includes your beliefs and experiences as well as the dramas that surrounded you in general such as TV soap nonsense and more specific situations within each area of your life. As an example, there is always a bully, hardman, or similar character in most TV shows. The effect of that is that you come to believe that bullies are always around and so you will then automatically adopt that belief as well as live life more cautiously. And on top of that, you may grow to see people as not being trustworthy.

That narrow view can then affect all areas of your life and limit your growth in all areas. What we see as being a normal part of life through TV and media is accepted as reality-based and causes a conflict between who we are and what we want to achieve. We begin to limit our choices of what is possible. We begin to doubt ourselves for fear of being harmed by one of these bullies or nasty mafia types. In short, we then empower the negative symbolism thrown at us through life as well as media and TV.

And as we have suggested several times now, we become a self-fulfilling prophecy and create more of what we fear, what we think about consciously and unconsciously. We attract more of it through the R.A.S.

Role-Playing
In each compartment of our lives, we develop roles within our identity that we then play out in our life. Of course, we can create good heathy and positive roles but when we associate a particular role to a specific drama that we either experienced or watched someone else experience we begin to live that role through the drama. We then accept the drama as being a normal part of life and the way we live that part of our life.

This is essentially a form of a limiting belief that we absolutely must remove less we want to live out the role for the rest of our lives unconsciously acting on that role and as that character would act. Being defensive and attracting people who also support the role are just a few examples.

Essentially, we should avoid or remove dramas that cause us to live out a particular role that blocks, limits, or takes away our internal happiness and instead seek activities that we consciously choose and that enhance our internal happiness at the same time removing the dramas and external stimulus that affect our state of happiness.

Holding onto the identity caused by the roles we play out can be difficult to let go mostly because the ego likes to experience the role, identity, or drama. Again, you will become a self-fulfilling prophecy when you identify with the role unless you take action to remove the external stimulus that supports the role or drama.

So, it's important to examine the roles you play and to then list the benefits that you experience due to that role being played out. What are you getting out of it? And the same thing can apply to all types of dramas in your life including illnesses that get people to show you attention, by playing the victim, and even hanging onto a poverty consciousness.

Positive Identity Roles That Serve You

So, what can you do about the negative roles you take on through your dramas and other life experiences? Well, a good place to begin is living a life of gratitude. Gratitude has a very high vibration and can begin to change you from the inside out. Simply by showing gratitude for the good things in your life helps you make the shift less painful from roles that don't serve your best and highest interests to roles that do serve you.

Of course, Eliminating the Negatives is a part of all of this so I highly recommend that program, but there are other steps that you can take such as living a life of purpose and meaning and even contribution. I personally believe that contribution is a natural effect of creating value for others but if you are not in your own business then simply being of value to others and society can often help make the shift from negative life experiences to more positive ones and of course with far fewer dramas and negative roles being allowed to force a particular role on you.

You can change a role simply by becoming aware of it and then making slight changes that cause bigger long-term results and positive experiences. You can simply create an affirmation to replace the negative role.

For example, let's say that the role you are playing out is that of a victim of government oppression. If that is the case you are constantly thinking or have taken on the limiting belief that, "the government is against me" … now ask yourself, is that really true? If you think about it objectively you will see that the government does a lot of good. Keeping us safe from those who would do us all kinds of harm being the most prominent role that they play. But they don't do this to oppress you. They do this to keep you safe from the ones that would do you harm.

So, take an objective look at your roles and see them as negative affirmations that you are constantly thinking, believing, and living. The government is against me, being an example.

In our example, instead of that oppressed feeling that comes with living the role of "the government is against me" create an affirmative statement that replaces the oppressive role such as, "the government does good things that support others and myself and keeps us safe from harm. I am grateful we have a government that doesn't force me to live against my will". That's just an example and I am sure you can come up with other statements for this example if you do suffer from that role, or for your own life experiences and negative roles that you play.

It's a vital point that you understand that all of this is defining and clarifying the person you want to become as covered in Your Three Life's main document, online program, and workshop. And by the way, I am aware that grammatically that title should be Your Three Live's, but that would be false in that you only have one life.

Your three Life's refers to the separation or disintegration of your one life in order to gain more control of yourself. First through knowing yourself better and second through defining and clarifying the "Who" that you want to be and that you are always creating and becoming for your good or bad.

And so, taking on this work is an essential yet often bypassed process that many neglects to take up and instead pursue instant gratification. They are trying to get to the destination by becoming who they need to be without putting in the effort to BE that identity that supports their success.

Another vital consideration is to realize that this won't happen instantly or overnight. However, once you begin to make these changes your mind may start to become clearer for brief moments once you get used to making these types of changes but as in our Heathrow to the Bahamas analogy, it won't happen overnight. It will become, over time. You will notice new realities beginning to open up for you on a very subtle basis if you observe what is happening around you, within you and because of your subtle pattern changes as you progress.

So, be patient with yourself and just KNOW, and have faith in yourself that the changes will grow. How can they not when you make these small yet great changes within yourself and your life?

Layer 4: It's All a Question of Time?

Time... what a subject. As a professional drummer, I became intimately acquainted with time, simply because a drummer's role is to create time. In the music world they call it "keeping time" or "timekeeping", but that isn't an accurate assessment of what time is.

That said, let me explain a little deeper. To understand this, you need to understand Your Three Life's concept of past, present, and future which is discussed within the full version only. The present being now. But the present and now are two very different concepts. The present refers to "what is" presently occurring in your life and around you. So, it is a larger perspective or "now". Now can be seen in any instance of the present. It is really a disintegration of the present.

Look at it this way, if the present was a centimeter, now is any point between the far left and far right of the measure. Now, is each millimeter taken in turn! Or each millimeter has chosen at a particular point within the centimeter. And of course, this is also expressed in the modern concept of a clock. We have hours, minutes, and seconds. So, "now" can be viewed as any one of those seconds whereas the present is really a perception of the wider hour and even the day.

So, you should begin to see that the present is a continuation of now.

This is important to understand yet it is only important for understanding in order to gain more control of our lives and nothing more. Returning to the drumming analogy, if a drummer is playing in 4/4 time which most modern music is written and played in, he doesn't play a note on one second, and then every 5, 10, 20 seconds depending on the speed of the music being played. He plays in intervals that don't fit into the seconds and the minute version of time.

So where does he play?

Well simply put, the drummer plays time at intervals that he creates through a prearranged tempo either given to him by a bandleader or created by himself.

When considering the seconds and minutes of real clock time when a drummer hits his first beat, when he plays his second beat, third beat and fourth beat, and so on... what happens is that time, or rather SPACE moves. So even though the drummer is still in the present, he is controlling the now and what he plays in that moment of now in order to produce an effect. Music. Or timing.

So, as we can see, time is movement and from a drummers' perspective time is really choosing points in space that are perceived external to himself as being timekeeping.

I was going to delete all of the last few paragraphs but then thought to myself that they hold so much value in the way of perspective that I would keep them in. You see, the drumming analogy explains or interprets time quite well but also those four or five paragraphs do exactly the same. From the point, I began to write the last five paragraphs until NOW, I have not changed but time passed as well as the space between the beginning and the end, the Alpha and Omega, you can then see that I created five paragraphs of writing. This could very well have been 5 drum beats. But I digress...

So, the importance of that explanation of time is to realize that time is movement. Space moves around you whilst you remain in the present and in every moment of now. It is what you do with the seconds that produce either an eventful minute or present or an uneventful one. Time is the most powerful concept and tool we can ever choose for ourselves whether we are eliminating dramas, eliminating negative bad habits or beliefs, creating better experiences and more joy, or building a business.

This all boils down to choosing to live a life of purpose or to waste your time. To live life on purpose or without purpose. But from our new perspective of time, we either move and ACT or, we stagnate into the reality that we allow to overcome us. Life then happens to us. We either grow or die. Of course, this kind of death is a wasted life and not actual physical death.

So, you could say that time is movement between birth and death. It is what we do with that movement, whether we move and act or stagnate and die.

Now, with the understanding of the Your Three Life's, it should be clear that these two versions for both you and I... the one who stagnates or doesn't move and the one who moves acts, and builds are constantly at war with each other. Neither wants the other to exist.

They are at war because the past which is static doesn't want you to become the Future you which is dynamic. Of course, this is another analogy but it serves the importance of continually building yourself and your life into the you that you want to become.

The past doesn't exist at all and is mostly just memories that are kind of static within us but they can grow and change also. Indeed, the past is expanding from the perspective of you or any other individual moving through time in the present or now. The memories are becoming more abundant and can in some cases be changed and adapted to better suit our individual current needs.

Quite literally we must look at time, choose what we want to become, act creatively to make it a new reality, build it, develop it, enhance it, become it then and be all of it in every new moment of now. That is the only way to live a new present moment that is more conducive and congruent with what you want to become.

The present and current you cannot handle the new life and success you seek if you are the ambitious type. That's because in most cases we strive for lives that are beyond our reach. And so, success is simply the journey to bridge that gap. To become the person we need to be, who can handle the success we seek in an almost effortless fashion. This is the real reason so many fail yet don't need to if they take on the journey and never give up until they become the new and better version of themselves.

Time Is of Vital Importance
Time is so important that I decided to keep the past several paragraphs in place as I write this to serve as a point of constant reference for you to eliminate the dramas and negative roles, habits, and other life experiences that are not serving you. You do all of that in the NOW. You cannot do it later, yesterday or tomorrow. It can only be done now. And it is your choice and your choice alone as to whether or not you do what needs to be done. This book serves as just a guide, but you absolutely must do the work on yourself if you want to improve your lot in life and build a better life experience for yourself.

So, now that we understand the playground or play area in which we create and build our lives, let us turn inward and discover how time can help us to gain more happiness.

The Turning Point
Up until now, everything that we have mentioned here has been concerned with external stimuli and situations within your environment and life. From this point forward, we will be more concerned with the internal part of our journey or perspective. But having said that, time is really a shifting point. A pivot if you will, from external to internal and internal to an external focus.

As previously mentioned, your playground or where you do everything that you do and feel everything that you feel is now. From this point, the past becomes just an impulse of memory and a vast array of energy where everything that you have ever experienced is archived. You can look at that past as being full of positive or negative experiences as suggested within Your Three Life's main documents.

We access that information by calling forth images of an event. These images are mostly still images but with a little practice, we can see the moving picture version. What's important in our journey towards more happiness is to transform that past into a positive experience so we can see our lives as being a positive experience. I go into this much deeper elsewhere, specifically within the Prelude to Upgrade Your Happiness Workshop that is available in the online version of this book.

But for now, it is sufficient to understand that through the actions we perform now we can begin to change the past through the actions and events that we do, create, and form now.

The now is always going to transmute into the past wherein 5 years' time we can either look back fondly at our creations or look with a disappointed eye whilst we think what we could have achieved if only we had made the effort. And of course, by being here now reading or listening to this you are making the effort.

From this same standpoint of now, we can focus on a future not yet created, and again we can look into that future positively in an expectant manner or we can look at it with a negative slant and so, experience that negativity in the now. And again, it is clear that we should look into the future, create what we want to exist in that future now, and then act in the present to enhance that future in a state of positive expectation which simply affirms that what will be, will be congruent with your desires. Your internally chosen and controlled desires.

Creating Your Own Experience

Our personal perspective or orientation can be focused on either experience or remembering. This essentially means whether we experience happiness now or are remembering the happiness of a past event. These two selves as we will call them are the experiencing self and the remembering self.

The Experiencing Self: thinks about the present, now, and wants to experience happiness and joy now. This happiness is usually experienced because of an event in the individual's current experience. It is essentially being at the effect of a previous cause or life occurrence that is usually outside of us.

The Remembering Self: experiences happiness and joy about life and lets past events that occurred form their basic level of happiness in the form of positive memories. The remembering self reflects on past experiences and feels joy from them.

This is evident in many life scenarios, but it is important to note that what is remembered can be either good or bad. For instance, in a relationship, let's say that a couple spends the day together doing some kind of activity. When they both recall that activity, they may both remember a completely different experience. One may remember the experience as a bad or negative experience whilst the other may look back on the event as being a positive experience.

Of course, the way in which the two entered into the event would make a difference in the remembered outcome as well as the specific events that occurred within the eventful day.

Another important observation is that when we remember we remember the beginning and end of something we experienced more than we remember the middle of that same experience. This is why when studying we are advised to take short breaks often, stretch your legs, take a brief walk, or simply stand and stretch. This is an accelerated learning technique that is quite powerful when learning any subject.

Walt Disney takes advantage of this idea at Disney world. You may have had to spend most of the day queuing for rides and other facilities but most people remember Disney world in a positive light. Why is that? It is because at Disney world at the end of the day they create a big party atmosphere with fireworks and other amusements to give the visitors a good memory when they leave Disney world. Visitors are much more likely to return if what they experience was a great day filled with happiness and joy.

So, if you want to look back on events fondly, simply finish on a high note. That way you will think about the experience as being better than it actually may have been.

This is an advanced concept as we discuss in the Eliminate the Negative program. If you don't eliminate the negatives then you take them with you into your future experience. So, this also suggests that choosing to be happy now and to finish holidays, day trips, and other life events on a high note simply because every moment of now is carried forward into your future now. This is the same as when a couple split up due to one or other of the partners' past. They have too much baggage... they brought those negative experiences from their past into their future where they were negatively judged or dumped due to the past experiences of the individual.

This concept is also just like limiting beliefs that were created in some past event or experience and are then constantly carried forward and left to affect the present, which then affects future outcomes as previously suggested.

Layer 5: Are You Against Yourself?

Negative patterns are something that we all have at one time or another and are usually the effect of a trigger that caused the pattern to begin. We can have negative response patterns to other people's body language, emotions, as well as other activities and learned behavioral responses.

Examining our lives to discover the triggers that cause us to act a certain way or perform a certain action is a vital part of self-improvement. We must discover what our triggers are and we can only do that by examining our behaviors and asking questions such as: what caused me to behave that way, what caused me to feel this way, and so on.

But again, it is important to note that our behavioral patterns can be either positive or negative patterns, productive or destructive to ourselves, our lives, and our happiness.

Creating A Happy Place

When we find ourselves in a negative state or situation that was caused by a trigger it's important to ask questions to uncover the trigger and it's also important to get into the habit of taking yourself to your happy place. Imagine yourself in a country setting, bathing in the ocean, laying on the beach, or whatever place you prefer to call your happy place.

Of course, you should create a happy place in your imagination and imagine it often so you are more easily able to call on your happy place at will when things get too much or too negative.

Your happy place can also be someone or something that you love such as your wife, your son, daughter, or a favorite activity, and so on. You can use this happy place in any form you like and you can use it in many situations that would normally get you down, angry, or depressed. Let's say for instance that someone you dislike for one reason or another, they bug you but then call to see you either by knocking on the door or by calling you on the phone, email, or other. Instead of getting angry and defensive simply take yourself to your happy place to eliminate what is obviously a negative life experience or event. Turn it around.

Of course, you don't wish the person any harm, but neither do you want them to put you in a negative situation or state of being.

And remember, what we focus on is what we see more of and what we think of is what we think about and then create more of it so you should get used to going to your happy place at will, just to make sure that what you are focusing on is beneficial for you, your life and your happiness.

Again, we fulfill our own prophecies through the R.A.S, this is the basis of forward-thinking and positive thinking but it is also important to eliminate the negatives and not simply go through life thinking of the positive things when we have negative situations that tend to steal our joy at various points in and throughout our lives.

So, make going to your happy place a part of your life to begin the process of eliminating negative states caused by external stimulus. And remember small changes can make a big difference.

Layer 6: How Do You Truly Feel?

Your state of being or mood is created from groups of emotions regarding each area of your life. But what are your emotions made of? We will get to that, but first understand that we must change our emotions regarding a particular life situation to begin to build a better state of being, mood, or happiness in a particular life area. And so, we need to uncover our current emotional states.

As I mention in the Eliminate the Negatives program, emotions are made up of collections of images related to a specific area of your life.

For example, if you are in love you don't simply see the other person as nearly perfect, they open the door for you, they get your coat when leaving a party, they open the car door for you, and so on.

These are just the effects of what is really going on within you. You see these things like the effects of your emotional state of being in love. But the emotion of feeling love is an effect of the combined images that you hold to be true for that person.

In any particular situation in any area of your life, you should be able to divide each of the feelings regarding that area of your life. Let's stick to the example of love even though this is a very difficult area to use as an example because many people believe love to be an intangible sort of energy. But for our example, we will stick to it as it is a clear cut, yet an extreme example of an emotional state.

So, you are in love with a particular person, that person opens the door for you when you enter a building, he or she, and we will stick to "he" in these examples, he moves the chair back when you sit for dinner, he opens the car door for you, he does this that and the other. Well, all of the actions or things that he does for you have become memories and associations related to that particular person whom you love. Each memory is built up from the moment you first met this person and each of those memories becomes an image or little movie that you play in your mind regarding each of the actions he performs for you and the way you see that person. You make a judgment or belief based on those images and experiences, good or bad.

So, each of those actions, images, or movies are associations of that person and so whenever you think of that person you immediately bring all of those associated images and movies together and the effect of those images is the emotion you feel, based on the belief you have created. I am not a chemist and so there may possibly be endorphins and other hormones released because of the feelings or associated grouped images... but the effect is still the same. When you hold an almost perfect collection of images associated with a particular person then that will produce a particular and specific effect. An emotional state.

Now, the interesting part is that you may, over time add images that either support your initial group of images or emotions or that downgrade the way you feel about a particular person. And as many people know, a single negative image can wipe out and completely destroy all of the positive memories and associations you hold of that person. An example would be if that person cheated on you, stole from you or anyone else, committed a crime, or other activity or action that went against your code of moral beliefs or ethics.

So, as you can see from all of this, visualizing your goals as taught by many self-improvement experts is not enough to create a better life experience. You have to feel that you already have the item you are visualizing and that is done by creating groups of images that relate to a specific outcome and that you feel strongly about. If for example, you happened to be looking for love, then you would create images of him or her, opening the door for you, moving the seat back as you sat for dinner, opening the car door for you, and so on.

The images that you chose to create will be directly related to what you believe love should look like for you.

The images then more easily allow the individual to experience the emotion of love. And because the brain doesn't know the difference between imagining something and it being real, It helps you to find more of that feeling or emotion. Of course, this is why when you state your goals, they must be very specific. Even exact.

So, we see that emotions determine your reality along with your focus.

Relationship Matters

And so, if or when you find yourself in a conversation with someone and you are really happy yet the other person is sad, or you are in a positive state and the other person is in a negative state it is always a good idea to make an effort to help the other person create a happier state within themselves. Moreso if this is a close friend or partner. The effects of a positive person and negative person meeting in a specific conversation or life event are that one remembers the conversation or event as being a good uplifting one and the other remembers it as a negative and somewhat depressing situation or event.

Of course, this is more appropriate and applicable when dealing with someone you have a long-term friendship or relationship with, simply because the negative person will build up a bank of negative memories about the positive *(to you)* event and come to associate the positive person *(you)* as being present in the... what they believe was a negative event.

I don't believe anyone should really care what others think of them, especially when we have no real control over that person. But we can at the very least make a little effort to change the negative views, perspectives, and filters that people see us through. And of course, this is more applicable in business situations but who's to say that relationships and friendships are any different? Each relationship has value to us as individuals and in most cases, there is always an exchange of values in all relationships whether emotional, personal, or financial as in business exchanges. Whether we like to believe it or not this is a natural part of how the brain functions and how we function as human beings.

The Physiology of Happiness

As emotional beings, we should take it on ourselves to try to gain as much control over our emotions as possible for many reasons that in the end serve us and our wellbeing. As an example of the importance of this, we can take a look at the emotion of anger. When we become angry for whatever reason the prefrontal lobe in our brains which is responsible for logical, analytical, and critical thinking processes gets shut down. The amygdala, emotional center, or the monkey brain then becomes prominent and so our decision making becomes flawed as our negative emotions are related to anger build and then takes away our capacity to think rationally.

Luckily, this process can be easily reversed by simply focusing on your heart, closing your eyes, and then taking a few deep breaths. The prefrontal lobe then gets switched back into activity and your thinking processes become clearer and you're more able to think rationally and make rational decisions and choices once again.

Anthony Robbins teaches that by simply standing in an upright manner and taking on the stance as a superman or superhero with hands-on-hips and head held high will actually begin to change your state. You begin to feel indestructible and invincible. Then crafting a smile on your face becomes much easier. And as we have learned, the brain doesn't know the difference between a false smile and a real one and so will release endorphins that make you feel happy naturally. This may also give you a rush of self-confidence as you stand like your favorite superhero. And of course, it would be wise to take some initial steps to relax before trying this exercise in emotional state and control for yourself.

The benefit of this is that it not only helps the brain release chemicals that bring on happiness but your critical thinking ability, as well as creative thinking ability, will increase too. And so, we begin to see that being happy can and does help us to succeed within ourselves and in our lives as we are better able to think more rationally which can only help our state of being and our success in life.

Cell Replication
When we smile, we release endorphins and other chemicals that make us naturally feel happy. As the chemicals move through our circulatory system our general mood changes and we begin to feel good. The interesting part of this process is that new cells are created through cell division with the same characteristics as the ones that contained the chemicals or emotions of happiness.

Cells are covered with millions of tiny hair-like follicles or receptors that take on the chemicals from the previous undivided cell. And again, in this, we see that we are very, very literally a self-created machine or mechanism, a self-programmed mechanism, or we are a self-fulfilling prophecy. As a cell divides from a point where we were in a state of happiness, the newly divided cells contain more of that happiness so this adheres to just about every other rule of the universe regarding growth. Everything is accumulative, meaning the more of one thing there is the more it will produce.

Put another way... we create our own happiness through our own choices and our decisions... and of course, our current state of happiness.

And don't forget... if cell division or meiosis creates like cells when feeling happy the opposite is also true. When we feel sad, we are creating more sadness within the cells. That this eventually leads to illness in one form or another is my guess?

This all points to the *above so below* axiom or put another way, the microcosm and macrocosm of the universe. Or, the smallest parts of the cosmos within us, our cells, are reflected in the whole being that you are. In other words, as your cells are replicated and transformed into happier cells so does your whole body gets transformed into a more positive version of itself. And again, this replication extends beyond yourself out into the larger external world and cosmos. When people are happy around you and so on.

Happy people attract happy people which supports the idea that happiness is infectious so what is happening within a person through cell division and transformation, that same thing occurs within the whole person and then out into the world by attracting like-minded people who also enjoy feelings of happiness and joy. Well, don't they say, "Birds of a feather, flock together"?

If all of this spreads throughout our minds and our emotions and thoughts... then does this spread out beyond our microcosmic universe of ourselves out into the world and beyond, and into the cosmos itself?

We may in fact be the creators of the universe that we live in. And with the idea of a multiverse, then everyone would live in their own self-created version of a universe with varying perspectives on everything.

It's a little beyond this book on happiness but it does, I hope, encourage the reader to take his happiness and level of joy more seriously into the futures of now.

The Creating Your Own Universe Program goes into the practical side of creating your own environment through your personal mindset and is in effect an extension of this particular program.

One last note before we continue. Gratitude is up there with love when it comes to vibrational forces at our control and so it can pay great dividends in happiness, joy, and peace to be grateful or learn to become grateful for everything in our lives and to come to the understanding that even the negative experiences and circumstances serve a purpose. That purpose is usually to learn as we begin to move beyond the negative situation or experience. See the Eliminate the Negatives Program.

Unleash Your Personal Happiness

As we have discovered throughout this document, there is a very specific process to uncover and unleash your personal happiness and joy. By beginning to work on uncovering your personal version of the six layers we have covered you will begin to create a state of being that is enviable.

As you progress through the layers you will uncover things about yourself that although you may have been aware you didn't realize that it was all under your own control. Once again, the six layers are:

1. **Desire** - What you truly want in each area of your life.
2. **Limiting Beliefs** - What you believe to be true about yourself and everything.
3. **Identity or ego** - The mind-created version of yourself.
4. **Time** - Allowing each moment to pass by you unchecked.
5. **Patterns of Behavior** - Personal patterns, programs, and processes.

6. **Emotional State** - Control and choice - Choosing happiness and Living in Gratitude.

To begin the process of upgrading your happiness simply follow the following six steps.

But first please understand that as you practice each step and progress through that particular step... it is very important to understand that each of the steps isn't just a simple process that you perform once in your life and then forget about it.

Each step may require continued effort over time and some more than others. So, do the work on yourself to create a better version of yourself and your life. You will have then taken the First Master Step (Preparations for success) to have a better life experience.

Here are the six steps.

1. Create a list of all of your desires in each of your life categories, why you want it, and what state you are trying to experience.
2. Create a list of all of your negative or limiting beliefs about each area of your life.
3. Turn all of your limiting beliefs into positive affirmations and relentlessly pursue an improved success identity. Within each area of life.
4. Bring yourself into the now at every moment and practice becoming mindful.
5. Turn your personal patterns around through affirmations and changing your thought patterns.
6. Choose to be happy in every moment.

As a final note, as you begin to work on each step read and reread the appropriate section or layer within this document to make sure that you don't miss anything on your way to the 2.0 version of you and your life.

A Final Note About Positive Thinking

In my writings, I negate positive thinking quite a lot and to instead eliminate the negatives. I do this mainly because it's much easier to focus on the positives when the negatives have been taken care of.

It should also be noted that positive thinking and affirmations aren't supposed to bring greater success in life and hence prove not to work at all. The purpose of positive thinking is to move in steps from a state of negativity into an increasingly positive state of being. Affirmations then help in this process by first slowing down the negative situations and then slowly bringing into being a better life experience. This has suggested is much easier when the negativ4es have been first taken care of.

This is why persistence is so valuable on your journey to greater success and happiness.

I wish you great success on life's path, whichever path you choose.

And I wish you greater happiness and joy in everything that you do.

Thanks for listening.

Andy Raingold

Did You Enjoy Reading Happiness Upgrade?

I would like to thank you for purchasing and reading this book. I hope you enjoyed it and that it provided some value to yourself and your life.

If you enjoyed reading this book and found some benefit in it, I'd love your support and hope that you could take a moment to post a review. I'd love to hear from you, even if you have feedback, as it will help me in ensuring that I improve this book and others in the future.

To leave your review I have made it as easy as possible for you. Just visit or click your preferred link below.

Click Here to Leave Your Review *(United States)*
https://www.amazon.com/dp/1913929736

Click Here to Leave Your Review *(United Kingdom)*
https://www.amazon.co.uk/dp/1913929736

Other Books by Andy Raingold

Attitude Advantage
Freedom from Addictions
Your Assertive Life
Attraction Master
Communication Master
Focused Concentration
Fast Learning Genius
Enhance Yourself and Your Life
Unlimited Energy
Set High Goals Then Reach Them
Reboot Your Metabolism
Mind Mapping Mastery Tips
Raise Your Personal Motivation
Easily Defeat & Dump Procrastination
Subconscious Programming
Tap into The Universe
Unleash Your Power
Creative Visualization
Your Perfect Memory
Your Unlimited Power
Strategies to Boost Productivity
How to Become an Effective Manifestor
Boost Your Self Esteem
Listen to Yourself

Visit www.upgradeyourhappiness.com for more books by Andy
Raingold or search Amazon for the titles above.

Free Books

First Level VIP: Mastering Your Destiny
Second Level VIP: Your Seven Step Goal Setting Workshop
Third Level VIP: 5 Ways to Develop A Mindset for Success

The above three levels of success each contain:

- **An initial free product.**
    - Mastering Your Destiny
    - Your Seven Step Goal Setting Workshop
    - 5 Ways to Develop A Mindset for Success
- **A Success Letter.**
- **Main Product/Subject Area.**
    - The Better Life Experience Program
    - Super Productive Power Funnels Program
    - Creating Your Own Universe Program

Each deal with a specific subject:

First Level: Knowing what you want. **LIFE PURPOSE**
Second Level: Knowing how to get there. **SETTING GOALS**
Third Level: Knowing how to act on the way there. **MINDSET**

Visit **FirstLevel.VIP** to begin a journey to find your life purpose.
Visit **SecondLevel.VIP** to set massive goals and master your life.
Visit **ThirdLevel.VIP** to create your own success mindset.

DISCOVER: Why Happiness Is the Key to Success!
"And What You Can Do About It to Achieve Greater Success in Life"

The 'Your Three Life's' Upgrade Your Happiness Online Version includes:

- The Main Your Three Life's Document (Plus Audio Version)
- **Foundations for Yourself, Your Life and Everything Else** (Video and PDF Document - 10mins)
    - This video takes Your Three Life's to a whole new level and illustrates the massive value.
- **How to Make Positive Thinking Work** (PDF)?
- **The Six Master Steps & Hypothesis of Success** (Video and PDF Document - 9 mins)
- Clearing the Path - **Prelude to Upgrade Your Happiness** (PDF Document and Online Workshop - 35mins)
    - Instantly Accessible Workshop
    - Two Interactive Worksheets
- **Upgrade Your Happiness** (PDF Document)

You can Upgrade to The Your Three Life's Full Upgraded Version Here>>>

The Online, Your Three Life's Happiness Upgrade is a Profoundly Powerful Collection of Concepts that will not only help you to gain a better understanding of your past and present but also how to **clear out your past** and then **upgrade your happiness** so you can <u>possess the most powerful tool at your command</u>. Personal Happiness - Many people think that they will get happy when they get what they want, but the truth is *they won't get what they want until they are able to create a state of true happiness within themselves at will.*

TRACK: Your Happiness Upgrade!
"Make Sure You Stay on The Right Track to Greater Happiness With the Upgrade Your Happiness Journal & Planner..."

When you have begun the process to upgrade your happiness it's a good idea to plan and then track your progress. The Upgrade Your Happiness Planner and daily Journal allows you to more or less guarantee greater success as you take your first steps into a better version of yourself and your life.

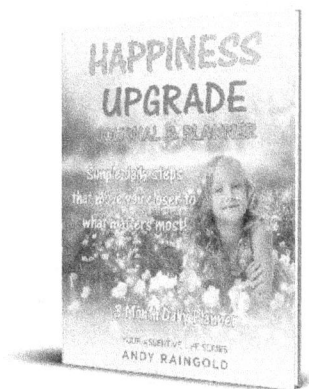

Visit www.upgradeyourhappiness.com to get the best start and the most beneficial results possible.

Please Note: The Upgrade Your Happiness Combined Planner and Journal is a 60-day process so it is a great idea to take advantage of multiple copies to continue your progress and enhance your happiness to the nth degree over time.

DISCLAIMER AND TERMS OF USE AGREEMENT

The author and publisher have used their best efforts in preparing this report. The author and publisher make no representation or warranties with respect to the accuracy, applicability, fitness, or completeness of the contents of this report. The information contained in this report is strictly for educational purposes. Therefore, if you wish to apply ideas contained in this report, you are taking full responsibility for your actions.

EVERY EFFORT HAS BEEN MADE TO ACCURATELY REPRESENT THIS PRODUCT AND Its POTENTIAL. HOWEVER, THERE IS NO GUARANTEE THAT YOU WILL IMPROVE IN ANY WAY USING THE TECHNIQUES AND IDEAS IN THESE MATERIALS. EXAMPLES IN THESE MATERIALS ARE NOT TO BE INTERPRETED AS A PROMISE OR GUARANTEE OF ANYTHING. SELF-HELP AND IMPROVEMENT POTENTIAL IS ENTIRELY DEPENDENT ON THE PERSON USING OUR PRODUCT, IDEAS, AND TECHNIQUES.

YOUR LEVEL OF IMPROVEMENT IN ATTAINING THE RESULTS CLAIMED IN OUR MATERIALS DEPENDS ON THE TIME YOU DEVOTE TO THE PROGRAM, IDEAS AND TECHNIQUES MENTIONED, KNOWLEDGE, AND VARIOUS SKILLS. SINCE THESE FACTORS DIFFER ACCORDING, TO INDIVIDUALS, WE CANNOT GUARANTEE YOUR SUCCESS OR IMPROVEMENT LEVEL. NOR ARE WE RESPONSIBLE FOR ANY OF YOUR ACTIONS.

MANY FACTORS WILL BE IMPORTANT IN DETERMINING YOUR ACTUAL RESULTS AND NO GUARANTEES ARE MADE THAT YOU WILL ACHIEVE RESULTS SIMILAR TO OURS OR ANYBODY ELSE'S, IN FACT, NO GUARANTEES ARE MADE THAT YOU WILL ACHIEVE ANY RESULTS FROM OUR IDEAS AND TECHNIQUES IN OUR MATERIAL.

www.ingramcontent.com/pod-product-compliance
Lightning Source LLC
Chambersburg PA
CBHW071621040426
42452CB00009B/1433